With God we live without God

*Reflections and prayers inspired by the
writings of Dietrich Bonhoeffer*

— MARTIN LIND —

TRANSLATED BY
SIGRID ELISE STRØMMEN

Sacristy
Press

Sacristy Press

PO Box 612, Durham, DH1 9HT

www.sacristy.co.uk

Swedish edition first published in 2017 by Argument, Sweden
English translation first published in 2018 by Sacristy Press, Durham

This English translation was supported financially by
Hilda and Håkan Theodor Ohlsson Foundation

Bible extracts, unless otherwise stated, are from the *New Revised Standard
Version Bible: Anglicized Edition*, copyright 1989, 1995, Division of
Christian Education of the National Council of the Churches of Christ in
the United States of America. Used by permission. All rights reserved.

Letters and Papers from Prison © Dietrich Bonhoeffer, tr. by Eberhard Bethge,
SCM Press, 1971. Reproduced by permission of Hymns Ancient & Modern Ltd.

Text of "By gracious powers so wonderfully sheltered" by Fred Pratt
Green (1903–2000) loosely based on the German of Dietrich Bonhoeffer
(1906–1945). English versification © Stainer & Bell Ltd. Adapted by
permission of SCM Press from Bonhoeffer's "Powers of Good", Letters and
Papers from Prison (1971). Reprinted by permission of Stainer & Bell Ltd,
23 Gruneisen Road, London N3 1DZ, England (www.stainer.co.uk).

Every reasonable effort has been made to trace the copyright holders
of material reproduced in this book, but if any have been inadvertently
overlooked the publisher would be glad to hear from them.

Sacristy Limited, registered in England & Wales, number 7565667

British Library Cataloguing-in-Publication Data
A catalogue record for the book is available from the British Library

Paperback ISBN 978-1-910519-93-6
Hardback ISBN 978-1-910519-99-8

Contents

Dietrich Bonhoeffer

The hour in which we pray for God's kingdom, is the hour in which we stand together with the world, an hour of clenched teeth and trembling fists. We do not in solitude whisper, "May we at least be blessed", but in our silence together we shout, "May this world, which has brought us together in dire straits, be over, and let your kingdom come!"

BONHOEFFER, 1932

Dietrich Bonhoeffer (1906–45) is one of the most well-known theologians of our times. More than seventy years after his death, he is still referred to in public debates, in discussions about solidarity and humanity, in conversations within the various Christian denominations, and in initiatives to unite the friends of Christ across the world. When ten statues of modern martyrs were unveiled on Westminster Abbey's West Front in 1998, Bonhoeffer was one of them. No one objected to this decision. Bonhoeffer was German, but had lived and worked in London for a few years in the thirties (1933–35), escaping the Nazi regime. He quickly made many close friends in Britain.

His writings cover a variety of themes and are still of great interest to contemporary scholars. Annual conferences attract scholars from all continents. Bonhoeffer is a well-known name where you might least expect it.

Here follows a brief summary of his intensive, 39-year-long life. He was born on 4 February in Breslau (now Wrocław in Poland), one of eight siblings. When Dietrich was six years old, his family moved to Berlin where his father, Karl, had been made Professor of Psychiatry. His mother, Paula, used her background in teaching to educate their children at home. Bonhoeffer grew up in a financially comfortable, middle-class, academic environment.

According to Professor Karl Bonhoeffer, the Church and theology belonged to the past. Although Paula's father and grandfather had been theology professors, he argued that in these modern times religion was outdated. Growing up with this example, it was far from apparent that Dietrich should later choose to become a theologian.

The death of Dietrich's older brother, Walter, was probably decisive in his later choice. Walter was fatally wounded after only a few weeks of serving in the First World War. When they learned of his death in 1918, the family was grief-stricken.

Bonhoeffer finished his basic education at an early age, thanks to his mother's tutoring. He chose the University of Tübingen to begin his theology studies, and a few months in Rome with his brother Klaus had a profound impact on him. There he became acquainted with the Roman Catholic Church and its adherents from all corners of the world. This was Bonhoeffer's first encounter with the global Church— quite a contrast from the insular, traditional Protestant environment he had known in Berlin. In Rome he discovered the true meaning of the word "Church". In those days this was a term barely accepted by German Evangelical theologians as it was considered to be a Roman Catholic concept. They preferred the term "Protestantism" to refer to Christians in other countries. What we now take for granted in a Church and a society with an increasingly global perspective in all aspects of life was a rare notion in Bonhoeffer's time. It was the nation state that was at the core of his contemporary society and Church. Thus, the global perspective of the Catholic tradition represented something entirely new to Bonhoeffer. The very word "Church" was like a beacon, or an ecumenical lever helping to create a widespread, unified theological community.

At the age of only 21, Bonhoeffer completed his Doctorate in Theology at the University of Berlin. His thesis was read throughout Europe and received instant praise, even from Karl Barth, the most reputed Evangelical theologian of the times.

Partly because of his young age, Bonhoeffer was encouraged to spend some time abroad. He spent the academic year of 1930–31 at the Union Theological Seminary in New York where he formed lifelong friendships. He was inspired by his studies and the discussions he had, and they proved decisive for his theological development. When he returned to Germany, the Nazis had tightened their grip on the country. His family had always been fervently opposed to Nazism, and when Hitler came to power in 1933, Bonhoeffer expressed his resistance in several ways. However, large parts of the German population and the Evangelical Church supported Hitler, and Bonhoeffer decided to move to London.

For nearly three years, Bonhoeffer worked as a German priest in London, where he made important connections, but eventually he was persuaded to return to Germany to head an anti-Nazi theological seminary. Higher education, now steeped in Nazi ideology, made it impossible for many of the remaining priests to contribute to theology programmes as their attitudes were tainted by a fundamentally positive attitude to Hitler. In Finkenwalde, in the north east of Germany, Bonhoeffer ran one of five theological seminaries for the so-called "Confessing Church" that opposed the Nazi regime.

In Finkenwalde Bonhoeffer further developed his theological thinking. Those years were perhaps the happiest of his professional life. Here his theological competence and creativity were combined with a pastoral programme and social fellowship. He met his best friend there, Eberhard Bethge, who would publish Bonhoeffer's writings after his death. He was able to pursue a life of prayer, meditation, and silence, as well as theological discussion and vibrant social interaction. But it was his regular times of silence every morning and evening, meditating on the Bible, which were the foundation of his daily life. Theology and faith could become one, a unity that became so important to him.

By the time the Gestapo shut down Finkenwalde in 1937, Bonhoeffer had completed a manuscript based on his lectures. The book entitled *Nachfolge* in German, *The Cost of Discipleship* in English, was widely read, even outside Germany. A shorter book, *Life Together*, with experiences from his life in Finkenwalde, also became widely acclaimed.

After Finkenwalde Bonhoeffer worked secretly as a theology teacher, leading weekend courses at various parsonages. Eventually the Gestapo shut down these sessions as well, and Bonhoeffer was given *Redeverbot*: forbidden to speak in public. He then withdrew and started writing what he considered to be his most important work: *Ethik* (Ethics). Sadly, he was never able to complete it, but the several hundred pages were published posthumously in multiple editions, in many languages.

In his last years he joined the resistance movement and was placed in the Abwehr, the military intelligence service. There was great tension and mutual suspicion between the police, the Gestapo and the Abwehr, and the Gestapo accused the Abwehr of undermining the Nazi regime. With hindsight we know that the Abwehr did in fact have several leading anti-Nazi agents in the organization. Bonhoeffer was placed in the Abwehr via these Nazi opponents within the organization.

Due to his placement in the Abwehr, Bonhoeffer was exempt from serving on the front. In the years 1940–43, he took part in several international missions run by the resistance movement under cover of official Abwehr work.

In April 1943 he was arrested and imprisoned at the Tegel prison in Berlin. Interrogations and investigations began and continued until the autumn of 1944. During his imprisonment at Tegel he was relatively free to work in his room—to read and to write. In this period he wrote a great number of letters, poems, hymns, and short stories. After his death a selection of his letters was published with the title *Widerstand und Ergebung*—known in English as *Letters and Papers from Prison*.

These eloquent letters are still read all over the world. Many of his reflections are open to different interpretations, and Bonhoeffer asks more questions than he gives answers in these letters.

Most of the letters are written to his friend Eberhard Bethge, but some of them are addressed to his parents. The letters to his fiancée, Maria von Wedemeyer, were not published until after her death, according to her wishes. These later letters are now available to the public, and are mostly love letters between the newly engaged couple.

Bonhoeffer was moved in 1944 to a much harsher confinement at the Gestapo's main headquarters on Prinz-Albrecht-Straße in Berlin. In the spring of 1945, the Nazis could finally prove Bonhoeffer's connections to the resistance movement, not to mention his role in the plan to assassinate Hitler on 20 July 1944. When this was discovered there was no way back. In February 1945 Bonhoeffer was secretly moved to Buchenwald concentration camp and then to the camp at Flossenbürg. He was sentenced to death by a court martial in the camp and executed on 9 April 1945. The leader of the Abwehr, Admiral Canaris, was executed on the same day.

The theological challenges, thought-provoking statements, and new intellectual constructs that defined Bonhoeffer's reflections are rendered in part in the following texts. Those who wish to study Bonhoeffer in more depth are naturally encouraged to look to the primary sources. What follows is a collection of thoughts inspired by one reader's reaction to his writings.

When I look through these finished texts, I see the extent to which my thoughts are coloured by my wife's struggle with illness and her later death. She died on 5 May 2016, on Ascension Day, during the same spring when I was working on this book.

Perhaps this has brought my writings closer to Bonhoeffer's own thoughts. A similar resonance may be heard in many of his writings. His reflections were also formed by his struggle, when faced by death, to come closer to life itself.

Martin Lind

Who am I?

Who am I? They often tell me
I step out from my cell
calm and cheerful and poised,
like a squire from his manor.

Who am I? They often tell me
I speak with my guards
freely, friendly and clear,
as though I were the one in charge.

Who am I? They also tell me
I bear days of calamity
serenely, smiling and proud,
like one accustomed to victory.

Am I really what others say of me?
Or am I only what I know of myself?
Restless, yearning, sick, like a caged bird,
struggling for life breath, as if I were being strangled,
starving for colours, for flowers, for birdsong,
thirsting for kind words, human closeness,
shaking with rage at power lust and pettiest insult,
tossed about, waiting for great things to happen,
helplessly fearing for friends so far away,
too tired and empty to pray, to think, to work,
weary and ready to take my leave of it all?

Who am I? This one or the other?
Am I this one today and tomorrow another?
Am I both at once? Before others a hypocrite
and in my own eyes a pitiful, whimpering weakling?
Or is what remains in me like a defeated army,
fleeing in disarray from victory already won?

Who am I? They mock me, these
        lonely questions of mine.
Whoever I am, thou knowest me; O God, I am thine!

FROM *LETTERS AND PAPERS FROM PRISON*

1. Every human life is irreplaceable

My soul thirsts for God, for the living God.

PSALM 42:2

Longing for someone can be a powerful feeling that occupies our thoughts, our dreams, even our whole life. In one of his prison letters to Eberhard Bethge, before his first Christmas in prison, Bonhoeffer writes, "In my experience there is no greater torment than longing" (18 December 1943).

It is not hard to imagine that someone in prison can feel an intense longing for other people, especially during the family festival of Christmas. You do not have to be in a prison cell, however, to feel a great longing.

When we are separated from someone we love, or when someone close to us falls ill and dies, it is natural to be filled with an intense longing for that person. There is perhaps no worse feeling than to be abandoned by someone who means a great deal to us.

Nothing can compensate for the absence of a person we love. We cannot turn other people into substitutes for someone we miss. No one can replace someone who is irreplaceable. God has made every human life irreplaceable.

In the Christian tradition, there is a risk that, albeit with good intentions, we point to faith in God as a replacement for the person we have lost. But God does not fill that void. God cannot be reduced to become a replacement for someone beyond our reach.

God leaves empty the void left by a missing person. This might sound harsh, but it is the only way. We must continue to live through our longing.

Memories, then, become important. They are like precious gifts we treasure deep inside. Now and then we can bring them out and be glad and grateful for them.

PRAYER

God, help me to live with respect for every human life
as a gift from you.
Let my longing for you make me love your gifts.

2. Time

How long, O Lord? Will you forget me for ever? How long
will you hide your face from me? How long must I bear
pain in my soul, and have sorrow in my heart all day long?

PSALM 13:1-2

Sometimes we perceive time as something empty. Ahead of
me are open days, hours, and minutes. It is up to me to fill
the time that awaits me. Each one of us fills the time we have
in our own unique way. But we also share many experiences
in life. We wake up, we wash, we eat, we read, we reflect, we
work, we socialize, we relax.

Bonhoeffer reflects on this in prison and decides to write
an essay on time, about our sense of time (*Zeitgefühl*).

Sometimes time carries with it an ambush. Seemingly for
no reason, without warning, an attack comes from nowhere,
stealing our time, invading and occupying the mind. It can
be called a *tribulation*, a word not often used today. But I
think we can all relate to this phenomenon. Suddenly matters
are brought to a head and the foundations of life start to
shake. Everything is laid open to doubt and we question the
meaning of life.

The effects of such difficult or dramatic experiences often
haunt us during the night. Bonhoeffer writes that he tries
to overcome these nocturnal tribulations by reading hymn
verses as a sort of shield.

Above the door in Bonhoeffer's cell, a predecessor had etched the words, "In one hundred years everything will be over". This was one man's attempt at surviving and enduring hardship. The psalms present two other perspectives. "My times are in your hand" (Ps. 31:15): a token of trust, something we can hold on to. But there is another way of seeing things: "How long?" (Ps. 13:1). It is often easier to relate to the latter.

When life is turbulent and our lifelines seem too fragile to hold, the question becomes acute: "How long? How long will you hide your face?" I find the image of the hidden face deeply moving. When no one sees me, when not even God sees me, it is as if I disappear completely. I long to be seen and appreciated as a human being. But more than anything, to be seen by God, by Life itself.

P R A Y E R

God, let your face shine upon me.

3. Despair

Out of the depths I cry to you, O Lord.

Lord, hear my voice!

PSALM 130:1-2

Among the sculptures of Ancient Greece, we find figures of great men, often with superhuman proportions, muscular, impressive, and seemingly radiating great pride and satisfaction.

One of the few exceptions is the statue of "Laocoön and His Sons".* When Bonhoeffer was eighteen years old, he spent a few months in Rome with his brother Klaus. They studied, learned more about the antiquity and the history of Rome, and enjoyed Italian culture. His encounter with Laocoön was striking.

Laocoön's face expresses deep despair. If you see the statue you will easily understand why: a man is holding his two sons close to him while venomous snakes are coiling around their three figures. He realizes that all hope is gone; there is no chance of survival.

Bonhoeffer recalls his first encounter with Laocoön and writes about it twenty years later in his prison cell. He thinks

---

* Laocoön was, in Greek mythology, a priest who warned against letting the Trojan horse into the city. He and his sons were suffocated to death by two giant snakes that arose from the ocean, which the Trojans interpreted as a sign that his predictions were wrong.

Laocoön's face may have inspired later images of Christ. Other statues in the Greek antique tradition hardly convey the suffering Christ.

The image of Laocoön is still a challenging sight. It is not easy to be confronted by depictions of great despair. I have also stood in front of the statue for a long time. The look of despair goes deeper and deeper. Inside all of us, there is a room in which despair, sorrow, and tears dwell. But we have become experts at keeping this room locked and its contents out of sight.

Perhaps we should rather help each other to open the door to this room. We should not strive to live in its infinite darkness. But we should have the courage to acknowledge that in my life there is a dark room, a room in which all I want to do is cry.

PRAYER

God, teach me to shed all the tears
so that there are none left.
You, giver of life, let me believe that you dwell in me
also in my dark despair.

4. Prayer in times of trouble

> Call on me in the day of trouble; I will deliver you, and
> you shall glorify me.
>
> PSALM 50:15

Times of trouble unsettle us and make our prayers desperate. This is human. In our greatest need our prayers are immediate and obvious.

Some people say that you should not name the same topic of prayer more than once when you pray. God knows all of our needs without us having to mention them.

For some, and I am one of them, praying in times of emergency is like a lifeline that I fill with the same old prayers.

Jesus himself tells the story of a person who knocks on his friend's door in the middle of the night. Because he is so persistent, the one who knocks shall have "whatever he needs" (Luke 11:5-10). God does not help us based on the number of prayers we lay at his door. I think the amount of prayers is more important to the one who is praying.

Many years ago I spent a few weeks on a personal retreat on the island of Patmos in Greece. Every evening I joined the sisters in their vespers in the convent named Evangelismos, or the Convent of the Annunciation. They followed the old order of prayer from the time of Chrysostomos. If I counted correctly, the plea "Lord, have mercy" (*Kyrie eleison*) was repeated twelve times. Every one of those pleas felt important to me. I was not concentrating on the number of times I repeated the words, but every time I joined in and appreciated them.

We are all different and we do not need to follow the same method of prayer. Nor do we need to assume the role of a kind of spiritual hero in which, purely based on our principles, we abstain from what we really want to do. Instead we can find rest in the inner order that grows out of each and every one of us.

PRAYER

In my need I call out to you, God.
You know me and everything about me
even before I begin my prayer.
Still I call out to you, again and again.
And I pray: Grant me whatever it is I need.

5. "Wishes, when we cling to them too tightly, can easily rob us of what we ought to be and can be"

LETTER TO EBERHARD BETHGE, 19 MARCH 1944

Give thanks in all circumstances.

1 THESSALONIANS 5:18

We all have desires and wishes. It is a natural part of being human. A whole life without wishes would be a deprived one. We imagine what the future might bring and we envision possible outcomes. Our imagination shows us that we wish for something more, we dream of something more, and we wonder what our life would look like if our wishes came true.

When Bonhoeffer, after almost a year in prison, reflects on this, he sees around him almost exclusively people who live entirely around their wishes. These friends are taking a risk. Clinging to wishes can occupy a person's world to such an extent that she cannot see beyond herself and her wishes for the future. She is no longer capable of being there for other people.

When I am preoccupied by what I want from the future I stop listening to others, I stop caring about other people. My own wishes claim all my energy and attention.

The alternative is to live as though we want for nothing else and to immerse ourselves in life as it is, here and now. The best remedy against allowing our wishes to consume us is the practice of gratitude. This is also God's greatest remedy against bitterness and sorrow. When we do not get what we want, we easily become resentful and impossible to be around.

Thinking instead about everything I am grateful for, however, makes room for something else. The air I breathe feels lighter and I soon start to see other people. And it becomes clear that I can give thanks for almost everything.

PRAYER

Open, God, the door to the room
that fills life with gratitude.
I need your help to stay there,
to meet myself and others.

6. "We are approaching a completely religionless age"

LETTER TO EBERHARD BETHGE, 30 APRIL 1944

> One God and Father of all, who is above all and through
> all and in all.
>
> EPHESIANS 4:6

Religion can mean different things. One common understanding stems from the idea that you can section off a person's life into religious areas, or rooms, that are different from non-religious ones. If you accept this view, all religious practices, such as church services and prayer, belong in the religious room while everything else—everyday life, work life, family life, cultural and social life—belongs outside this room. A narrow section of life belongs to what we define as specifically religious, while the majority of a person's life has nothing to do with religion at all.

A premise for this view is that "God" can be reduced to an object that human beings can control and stow away into a corner of life. For instance, God can have nothing to do with our work life or with the political life. This kind of division has been practised in totalitarian and communist regimes up to our own times, and it may even be detected in the rhetoric of the so-called "Christian right" in the United States today.

To Bonhoeffer this is a foreign notion. He seeks an interpretation of human existence in which God and Christ are present in everything, including the non-religious and worldly spheres. He advocates that Christians should belong to the real world, and live as God's workers in that real world, though at that point in his life, he is not yet fully aware of the consequences of doing so.

Perhaps we today—seventy years after his death—are also unaware of what this entails. But it seems that every age and every situation must find its own answers. What is most important is not whether we always get it right, for we will often fail, but that we keep trying, again and again.

For Christians this means allowing God to be God, and humans to be humans.

PRAYER

God, you were in my life before I could think or speak,
just as you are present in the whole universe.
Help us to see our responsibility as human beings,
as your workers, in all of life.

7. "Belief in the resurrection is not the 'solution' to the problem of death"

LETTER TO EBERHARD BETHGE, 30 APRIL 1944

Jesus said to him, "I am the way."

JOHN 14:6

We often say that the only thing we know for certain about the future is that we are going to die. Everything else is unknown and unpredictable. Many of us are reluctant to talk about death, and we run away from any thoughts concerning the end of life.

We are allowed to be afraid of death. It is natural that the unknown is unsettling to us. No one who has died has been able to tell us about it. And so an ominous cloud hangs over the subject.

Sometimes the Christian tradition has concentrated on the things that are beyond human comprehension and control. People have tried to reserve that which is beyond our realm of control to God. Because humankind cannot discover and understand absolutely everything, there are still areas in which God can conceivably exist and reign. In doing so, we place God at the outer margins of life, and God's "areas" are shrinking as human discovery expands and includes more and more.

The very idea of placing God at the margins is questionable. Bonhoeffer searches for God in the centre of everyday life.

It is in these places we need God. It is in these places we live in God's love. We can still cry out to God in our despair and vulnerability. But God does not only exist in these extreme places.

What then of death and our fear of dying? We know nothing about what happens when we die. This is why we must let the inexplicable remain unexplained. There is no need to speculate endlessly about what we cannot understand.

My belief is that our faith remains steadfast throughout all parts of life, both in the unfathomable and in the fathomable. My belief is that God takes care of us when we die, just as God takes care of us every day and every night of our earthly life. The resurrection is a manifestation of this care. But it offers no "solution" to the problem of death that faces me in life. Our Christian faith should help us turn away from death and look to those around us. This is where I find life; this is where I find those who need me now. This is where I may live with Christ.

PRAYER

God, help me to think less about my own death;
let me rather be your instrument of loving-kindness
as long as I live.
After life, I will throw myself into your caring arms.

8. "What is beyond this world is meant, in the gospel, to be there *for* this world"

LETTER TO EBERHARD BETHGE, 5 MAY 1944

> For a child has been born for us, a son given to us;
> authority rests upon his shoulders; and he is named
> Wonderful Counsellor, Mighty God, Everlasting Father,
> Prince of Peace. His authority shall grow continually, and
> there shall be endless peace for the throne of David and
> his kingdom. He will establish and uphold it with justice
> and with righteousness from this time onwards and for
> evermore. The zeal of the Lord of hosts will do this.
>
> ISAIAH 9:6–7

Our Christian faith should not tempt us to flee from our world in the hope of a better world to come. The Swedish protest singer Joe Hill, who was most likely wrongfully sentenced to death in the United States, wrote the famous chorus, "You'll get pie in the sky when you die." It might seem obvious to many people but it is not so easy to let go of this idea. For a long time Christian teaching focused on life after death.

This is hardly ever the message of the Bible. More often we see the opposite; the divine is anchored to the earth. According to the Hebrew Bible, humankind is created and kept alive by God. And God sends the Prince of Peace to show us the way to true life.

Bonhoeffer asks outright: "Does the question of saving one's soul even come up in the Old Testament?" He claims that everything in the Bible relates to a God on Earth, a God that comes to the aid of human beings.

Whichever way we interpret "saving one's soul", it is clear that the Bible advocates living here and now, in love and in truth. Nothing is more important than our current life. We most certainly need to be saved, to be "redeemed", from all the evil that threatens our life. But we also need to be saved from all attempts to flee from our own reality.

Our duty is not to dream of "pie in the sky" but to live life serving others. In this sense, Christian faith has something important to offer; it offers a fundamental perspective that sees human life as something great. All human life has divine roots. We could say that a human life is greater than itself.

PRAYER

Show me, God, the way to life.

9. "By gracious powers so wonderfully sheltered"

HYMN BY BONHOEFFER

Guard me as the apple of the eye;
hide me in the shadow of your wings.

PSALM 17:8

One of the last communications from Bonhoeffer is the letter he wrote to his fiancée, Maria von Wedemeyer, just before Christmas 1944. At that time Bonhoeffer was imprisoned in the cellar of the Gestapo headquarters on Prinz-Albrecht-Straße in Berlin. The letter contains a New Year hymn with the words, "By gracious powers so wonderfully sheltered, and confidently waiting come what may, we know that God is with us night and morning, and never fails to greet us each new day".

Bonhoeffer reflects further on these thoughts in the letter. He does not feel forsaken. Instead, he thinks of all the kind people close to him, of their prayers and good thoughts; he thinks about conversations, pieces of music, books. All good things that clearly protect and comfort him.

Bonhoeffer is not thinking primarily about God's protection in his letter. God's protection, though, is continually found in the loving care and kind thoughts of those around us.

It is easy to see God and humans in contrast to one another. But to Bonhoeffer the two go hand in hand. We do not need to construct a binary opposition, much less a competition, between the human and the divine.

My view is that humankind essentially belongs to God. All the "gracious powers" of creation spring from God's love. There are, however, other powers that continually seek to break us apart, to disturb and destroy our trust. This is why we need to encourage each other to see the gracious and the good in life. These shelter us, they uplift us, they open for us new worlds, again and again.

The gracious powers referred to in Bonhoeffer's hymn are signs of God's grace, the grace that awaits us every morning. Being given a new day to live is a precious gift. Some of us only truly realize this when illness and catastrophe disrupt our lives.

But it is equally true when life feels easy! Every day I receive life.

PRAYER

Teach me, God, to nurture life's gracious powers.
Let me help other people to receive your loving care.
Show me, Lord, your love every day,
so that I may receive and draw life from your daily gifts.

10. "This-worldliness must not be abolished ahead of its time"

LETTER TO EBERHARD BETHGE, 27 JUNE 1944

> Then Jesus went with them to a place called Gethsemane; and he said to his disciples, "Sit here while I go over there and pray." He took with him Peter and the two sons of Zebedee, and began to be grieved and agitated. Then he said to them, "I am deeply grieved, even to death; remain here, and stay awake with me."
>
> MATTHEW 26:36-38

When difficult things happen to us, we often feel uncertain as to what to do. It could be an unexpected piece of news that suddenly alters your life. It could be a fatal illness. It could be a person breaking up a relationship and leaving you. Personally, I think abandonment is the hardest sorrow to face.

There are no simple solutions to our despair, no quick fixes. Christian teaching can sometimes appear to offer us easy solutions. "If only you believe in Jesus enough, everything will be all right", we have been told. Those might not have been the exact words, but it is the essence of the message as we remember it.

But the Bible provides no shortcuts. Believing in Jesus is not an emergency exit from our anxiety and despair. Not even Jesus had an emergency exit from his grief and pain. We must, like Jesus, "drink the cup of earthly life". We too must live through our darkest hours.

What distinguishes our Christian faith is precisely the fact that it is directed towards our earthly life. When we affirm that life is stronger than death, that God gave life to Jesus at Easter, we may also hope that God will take care of us when we die. But this very hope brings us back to our present life, again and again. There is no need to live in anguish when faced by our mortality. God takes care of us in death. But at the moment, now, we have to live this life, the life that God gives us every day. That is our duty.

The life we have been given will not be ended before its time. We cannot evade the difficult challenges that continually demand our presence by escaping into life after death. To do so is to escape reality. It is trying to escape from God, who is with us every day of our earthly life.

PRAYER

God, teach me how to live now,
not yesterday, not tomorrow.
But right now.

11. When pushed away from public life, God was left to the personal, private sphere. God could only be important deep inside, where we are at our most vulnerable.

AFTER BONHOEFFER, 8 JULY 1944

> Mary said, "He has shown strength with his arm; he has
> scattered the proud in the thoughts of their hearts. He has
> brought down the powerful from their thrones, and lifted
> up the lowly; he has filled the hungry with good things,
> and sent the rich away empty."
>
> LUKE 1:51–53

In her "Song of Praise", Mary sings of a God that is active in society. She describes God's actions with brutal honesty. To Mary it is clear that everything in the world rests in God's hands. We might ask why God does not intervene and impose justice in our world today. We do not have a sufficient answer to the age-old question of how a good God can allow bad things to happen. But we all have a responsibility to contribute to God's justice being served. In this task, we can call ourselves God's workers.

Trying to isolate God within the personal sphere, the private sphere, does not only compromise the Christian faith. It threatens our lives. We risk letting the public sphere, society, the political and cultural life, become spheres that are beyond God's loving care. People then have to find their own set of rules and attitudes, or in the worst case live carelessly and indifferently. Historically, this has had devastating consequences.

When Bonhoeffer was in prison in the 1940s, the Nazis were in power in Germany. Some of their most fervent supporters claimed precisely this: the Christian faith should remain outside the public sphere. Politics and culture should remain in the hands of the Nazi leaders. Christian ethics and faith should not be practised publicly.

Today we still see similar tendencies from authoritarian positions. After all, it is so much easier for injustice to prevail when it is undisturbed and unchallenged.

With Christians throughout the ages, Mary is reminded that God already exists in society, in political, and in the cultural life, and that God is there waiting for us to work together in bringing justice to humankind.

PRAYER

God, open my eyes and awaken my courage,
so that you may use me in the fight for your justice.

12. "There is no need to go spying around for sins. Nowhere does the Bible do this"

LETTER TO EBERHARD BETHGE, 8 JULY 1944

> As he approached the gate of the town, a man who had died was being carried out. He was his mother's only son, and she was a widow; and with her was a large crowd from the town. When the Lord saw her, he had compassion for her and said to her, "Do not weep." Then he came forward and touched the bier, and the bearers stood still. And he said, "Young man, I say to you, rise!" The dead man sat up and began to speak, and Jesus gave him to his mother.
>
> LUKE 7:12–15

When we first meet someone new we rarely try to discover her flaws and shortcomings. Instead, we try to establish a common ground of trust that makes our encounter and conversation meaningful. We know that people grow and develop when they feel appreciated and when they are shown trust. Constant criticism, on the other hand, is suffocating and belittling.

Jesus does not begin by telling people about their weaknesses or their mistakes. According to Luke, when he met the widow of Nain he was filled with compassion. It is not even stated that the widow asked him to help her. Nor is there any information about the widow's sins or the son's moral life. Jesus sees someone in need. That is enough.

The Christian tradition has not always followed Jesus' example. The opposite has often been the case: old sins and guilt have come first.

This is a question of how you see people. We need to start seriously cultivating a Christian view of humanity, one that reminds us that all people belong to God. We need to learn from how Jesus meets people in the stories of the Gospels. Perhaps we also need to adjust our church services to accommodate such a view.

We begin by establishing trust. We begin by trying to approach each other, and God, in openness and in faith.

PRAYER

God, you know me better than I know myself.
Before your eyes I never need to disguise myself.
You know everything, great and small.
You know my strength but also my weakness.
Now I pray: Bless me so that I may
    grow to be what you want.

13. There is no such thing as "the inner life". The outer and inner life are connected in *all of life*

AFTER BONHOEFFER, 8 JULY 1944

> Jesus said, "Which is easier, to say to the paralytic: Your sins are forgiven, or to say: Stand up and take your mat and walk? But so that you may know that the Son of Man has authority on earth to forgive sins"—he said to the paralytic—"I say to you, stand up, take your mat and go to your home." And he stood up, and immediately took the mat and went out before all of them.
>
> MARK 2:9–12

The Bible does not differentiate between a person's inner and outer life. Jesus is clear on this point. He forgives the inner sins that are invisible to others at the same time as he relieves the same person from his outer, visible illness. And he makes a point of demonstrating the connection between these forms of redemption.

People of Christian faith lived for over a thousand years before we began to speak of a person's inner life. It is a product of the Renaissance, according to Bonhoeffer.

In the Bible everything is connected. "The heart" is not something deep inside but a whole person as she stands before God. Our lives are lived in both directions: "from the outside" and "inwards", and at the same time "from the inside" and "outwards".

Why is this an important distinction? Because what is so liberating about this discovery is that it means God cannot be shuffled away to a secret chamber of our innermost, invisible life. This is something we have already tried to do, perhaps from a fear to face God out in the open. Keeping God in the invisible places can seem more comfortable to us. We can avoid being bothered by God in our everyday life. God then exists in "religious" practices, in prayer and in church, and only there.

But this attempt to place God out of sight is futile, doomed to fail. It is also misleading, as it allows people to think that they can have an inner life completely untouched by their outer life. If we keep God in this protected, invisible room, all will be well.

But we live life with both an outer and an inner presence, invisible and visible, interwoven and inextricably linked. Our whole life is lived before God.

PRAYER

God, unify my life into something whole.

14. A human life is greater than itself

> When I look at your heavens, the work of your
>   fingers, the moon and the stars that you have
>   established; what are human beings that you are
>   mindful of them, mortals that you care for them?
> Yet you have made them a little lower than God,
>   and crowned them with glory and honour.

PSALM 8:3−5

The rapid development of the western world has placed human beings at its centre. Human inventions and human discoveries have paved the way for an incredible shift in our existence.

The Christian Church has to a certain extent always warned against emphazising human greatness—as if from a fear that God might fall short when compared to human achievements. This view stems from the idea that life is a competition between the human and the divine.

To Bonhoeffer such a competition is pointless. Humans belong to God who created us in the beginning. The great battle of existence is not between human and God, but between God and the devil, or God and evil.

This is not to imply that we as humans can turn a blind eye to our own shortcomings, for they are many and plain to see. What it means is that we have a duty always to lift up humankind. Where people are praised, God is praised. For Jesus is both true God and true Human.

We are not born as superheroes but as feeble infants left to the mercy of other people. The greatest danger a baby faces is abandonment. If a baby is abandoned, it will not survive. Perhaps abandonment is the greatest threat to anyone; I am more and more convinced of this. This is why Jesus on the cross cries out, accusing God of having forsaken him. If God has abandoned you, everyone has. There can be no worse predicament.

As humans we are carried by the life that is given to us freely, every day, every night. That life makes me greater than myself. That life unites every single person with God and humankind, with everyone. That life unites every individual with all of creation, the universe, the stars, the moon, and the sun, with every growing thing, every living creature, everything in existence.

This is why every human being is greater than herself. She does not need to believe in God to feel that this is true.

PRAYER

God, thank you for the life you give us freely,
expecting nothing in return.

15. "God turns towards the very places from which humans turn away"

LETTER FROM BONHOEFFER TO HIS

PARENTS, 17 DECEMBER 1943

> While they were there, the time came for her to deliver her
> child. And she gave birth to her firstborn son and wrapped
> him in bands of cloth, and laid him in a manger, because
> there was no place for them in the inn.

LUKE 2:6–7

In a stable among the animals, where human beings are not intended to live, much less give birth, God allows Jesus Christ to be born. It is not a romantic episode in a beautiful narrative, though many of us have grown up with the stable crib as an almost essential part of our Christmas scene.

According to Luke, the birth of Jesus was far from picturesque. Mary and Joseph had nowhere to stay and the stable in which they were eventually housed was a place of the utmost poverty—a location surely no one would choose for the birth of a child.

The information provided by Luke is not arbitrary. Misery, suffering, poverty, loneliness, helplessness, guilt—they all take on another meaning in the Christmas story. Jesus is born outside society, and the narrative shows God's presence in human need and in times of crisis. In all situations and places where no one wishes to dwell, there we find God.

Bonhoeffer reflects on this in the days leading up to his first Christmas in prison. According to him, a prisoner grasps the Christmas story better than most people. Jesus' birth in a stable transcends the limits of time and space, and renders the prison walls insignificant.

God turns towards the places from which humans turn away. This is not a criticism of our longing for fellowship and pleasant surroundings. We do not need to feel guilty about wanting these things. It is rather an affirmation of God's presence in the difficult places, in the places where I am weak and vulnerable.

PRAYER

God, I know there is no escaping
dark and difficult places in life.
When I find myself there, I have only one option:
to try to persevere, little by little.
I pray, God, never let me go, hold on to me.
Let me believe in your presence, even in those places.

16. Blessing

> Blessed are those who trust in the LORD, whose trust
> is the LORD. They shall be like a tree planted by water,
> sending out its roots by the stream. It shall not fear when
> heat comes, and its leaves shall stay green; in the year of
> drought it is not anxious, and it does not cease to bear fruit.
>
> JEREMIAH 17:7–8

Sometimes we can feel envious of people who seem to get more than they really need. But when we see things more clearly, we soon realize that our envy is uncalled for. No one, it seems, avoids suffering, setbacks, betrayal. It is naïve to envisage a person without both the good things in life and the things that are not so good.

In the Hebrew Bible God's love for humankind is often expressed with the term *blessing*. Today this word is perhaps a bit old-fashioned, but I think most people still find it has a pleasant ring to it. Who would not wish to be blessed?

Bonhoeffer writes to his friend Eberhard Bethge (28 July 1944), "This blessing is the addressing and claiming of earthly life for God, and it contains all [God's] promises." But this blessing never ignores the cross. To be blessed does not grant you a superficial life of ease. It encompasses everything and cannot be reduced to become something that lets us off all worry and care. God's blessing is much deeper.

The tree in Jeremiah gives blessing a depth, with strong and reliable roots in the ground. Jeremiah gives us an image of roots drinking water from a source deep beneath the surface. Someone who is blessed can be seen as someone who has found a deep, hidden source, invisible to others, but strong and everlasting.

Is not this, to receive God's blessing, the very essence of the Christian faith? To live a blessed life, never turning away from the cross, but always anchored in the depths of life, in life itself, in our trust in God.

PRAYER

Bless me, God!
Open my life to your blessing
so that I may remain steadfast by your side.

17. "Later on I discovered, and am still discovering to this day, that one only learns to have faith by living in the full this-worldliness of life"

LETTER TO EBERHARD BETHGE, 21 JULY 1944

Let the same mind be in you that was in Christ Jesus.

PHILIPPIANS 2:5

Our most important task is to remain present in the earthly life we share as fellow human beings. Our Christian faith helps us to live in this way, to avoid escaping reality to the fantasy world that exists only in our daydreams. Our Christian faith is connected to this life, here and now. And our guide is Jesus, who was a human being.

We all escape from reality now and then. This can be harmless; it can even be a delightful refuge that restores us. We do not need to feel guilty about daydreaming. No human being is carved in stone; we all have dreams and wishes.

This is not, then, an attack on daydreaming. And Bonhoeffer would certainly not criticize literary fiction. Indeed, literary depictions can shed a new and exciting light on life.

Instead, it is a question of what I place at the centre of my life. If I try to centre my life around the idea of a world after death, I risk neglecting my earthly life. There is a great risk that we see our earthly, everyday life as a waiting room to the actual life that awaits us in heaven. These are the dreams we should let go. They distort our life in this world.

Jesus is our guide. He took his life on earth extremely seriously; he sacrificed everything for it. When faced by death and resurrection, we must still live, here and now. As friends of Jesus, as workers of God. The unconditional love that Jesus shows us can fill us with renewed courage and life, forever and ever.

PRAYER

Let me, God, live the life you give me every day,
honouring you and thankful for your gift.
Help me to remember that everything
    I experience has one ultimate goal:
to live here and now, doing your work.

18. We do not believe in a God that solves all problems

> Jesus said, "And remember, I am with you always, to the
> end of the age."
>
> MATTHEW 28:20

It would make life much easier if we believed in a God that solves all our problems for us. This kind of God was commonly depicted in the theatre of Ancient Greece. A mechanical device sent a god flying onto the stage to save the day. It was called a "god from the machinery" (*deus ex machina*). This was often seen as a portrayal of the divine as a force that offers simple ways out of tricky situations.

In one of his prison letters (30 April 1944) Bonhoeffer writes that he sees in his time an attempt to appeal for a *deus ex machina*, to let God simply rush on stage when you feel like giving up. But this is a superficial solution to our problems, or it is an attempt to find a power to fill the void where humans fall short.

The Bible does not present us with a God that solves all of our problems. God did not send Jesus to save us from our problems, from difficult situations. Jesus has another mission.

To put it bluntly we could say that we have been left to ourselves to find our own solutions to the dilemmas and difficulties of life. We have no emergency button we can push that will save us with straightforward answers and easy exits. At least not in the Bible.

Christianity offers something else entirely. According to Matthew, the last words of Christ were, "I am with you always, to the end of the age." This is not a promise always to find the way for us when we are lost. It is a promise of divine presence.

We get into trouble, we make mistakes, we fall ill, we die—our Christian faith does not tell us that this can be avoided with more prayers and piety. Our Christian faith underlines the fact that bad things happen to every single one of us. Christianity offers one answer: no darkness is so black that God is not with us there.

PRAYER

God, grant me insight into your presence;
help me to surrender my life to you, in trust.

19. "It is not necessary that we should discover new ideas in our meditation. Often this only diverts us and feeds our vanity"

LIFE TOGETHER, P. 63

> And all who heard it were amazed at what the shepherds told them. But Mary treasured all these words and pondered them in her heart.
>
> LUKE 2:18–19

As an adult Bonhoeffer began a practice of daily meditation. He read some words from the Bible and let them settle in silence. It was a ritual that was significant for his theological reflections. In this context he warns against striving for new ideas every time you meditate.

Mary is an example. She pondered the words in a hidden place in her heart. Meditation is a way of getting in touch with ourselves, with the depths of life, with God.

It can be tempting to expect some sort of special experience, surprising and unique, when we retreat in silence to meditate. More often than not, however, we find the absence of such an experience. Many people feel instead an emptiness and aversion, even indifference. Bonhoeffer's advice is to continue with perseverance and regular practice.

Through patience and practice, we learn how to grow and become closer to ourselves. To demand a special experience is in many ways a sign of immaturity, and perhaps a fear of truly facing ourselves.

We should not take our negative experiences so seriously. Meditation is not primarily about regarding ourselves in a mirror. It is a way of getting closer to life. In doing so, we must gently and decisively focus on the Bible words that are the object of our meditation. "'Seek God, not happiness'—this is the fundamental rule of all meditation. If you seek God alone, you will gain happiness: that is its promise."

PRAYER

God, teach me how to meet life in silence.
Let me rest in your love and your presence,
so that I may find courage to live for others.

20. Who am I?

> Let us love, not in word or speech, but in truth and action.
> And by this we will know that we are from the truth and
> will reassure our hearts before him whenever our hearts
> condemn us; for God is greater than our hearts, and he
> knows everything.
>
> 1 JOHN 3:18–20

We can never fully know who we are. Just as I cannot always comprehend other people, I cannot always comprehend myself. Every so often we wonder why we thought what we thought and why we did what we did. And we can't quite explain it. But the Christian faith offers a liberating view. Only God "knows everything".

Even in a close relationship one might burst out to the other, "How can I love you when you don't even know me?" But we have then turned our companion into our God, and no one can carry that burden. This is why it is so liberating to believe that God and only God can fully know who we are.

In his prison cell in the summer of 1944, Bonhoeffer writes the poem "Who am I?" He questions whether he really is all the things other people claim he is. He hears that people perceive him as calm and even cheerful, that he talks freely and is friendly with the guards, almost as if he were the one in charge. It was said that he, in the midst of his hardship, seemed serene and proud, like someone accustomed to victory.

But on the inside he feels uneasy, caged in, as if gasping for breath, as if he is being strangled. He longs for human closeness, he feels powerless, empty, and weary, ready to take his leave of it all.

Who is he? Is he either or both?

You do not need to be in a prison cell to question who you are. Most of us carry different images of who we are. Sometimes the images that come from outside are less positive than those of Bonhoeffer. But I still think that the harshest images of ourselves are the negative ones we carry inside.

Bonhoeffer ends his poem without providing any answers. The only thing he knows is that God knows him, and that he belongs to God.

PRAYER

You, God, truly know me.
Let me live my life trusting that I belong to you,
every day and every night,
every day of my life, and the day that I die.

21. "Only when one loves life and the earth so much that without it everything seems to be lost and at its end may one believe in the resurrection of the dead and a new world"

LETTER TO EBERHARD BETHGE, 5 DECEMBER 1943

> For the whole law is summed up in a single commandment,
> "You shall love your neighbour as yourself."
>
> GALATIANS 5:14

There is no higher aim than to give one's life to others in love. This may seem obvious and facile. But everyone who has tried to do so knows that it is a lifelong project, and that it is far from easy.

The most important thing is not to overlook the people we meet in order somehow to please someone else. And we should certainly never overlook God, thinking we can please God by trying to love our neighbour.

The last point is, of course, true, but it is not a case of using other people as a means to achieve some other end. The Bible states that we must love both God and our neighbour. This is not an encouragement to become cross-eyed, to look in two opposite directions at once. God's commandment is this single one: "You shall love your neighbour as yourself" (Mark 12:31).

To use people as an object of our love hoping to score points on some heavenly scoreboard cannot be called true love. In love there is nothing beyond the person we love, nothing else we should be striving for. Love sees only those in need of our care, our consideration, our forgiveness.

The will of God is undivided. In all of existence God assigns us one single mission. We do not have a different mission for when we are at work, out in society, and in the family. In all parts of life, we have the same mission.

A Christian faith does not make our life project any smaller. Rather the opposite. A Christian faith emphasizes and gives us no choice: You shall love your neighbour! And when you do this with all your heart, allowing your whole life to be filled with this love, you can trust that God will take care of you when you die, give you new life, a new world in love.

It is a question of directing your efforts in the right place. The aim of my life is to be there for others. If I let this define my life, I may also hope that God will take care of me when I die.

PRAYER

Let your will, God, direct my life,
so that I may believe that you are with me,
even at the end of my earthly life.

22. "Cheap grace is the deadly enemy of our Church"

THE COST OF DISCIPLESHIP, P. 35

> How precious is your steadfast love, O God! All people may
> take refuge in the shadow of your wings. They feast on the
> abundance of your house, and you give them drink from
> the river of your delights. For with you is the fountain of
> life; in your light we see light.
>
> PSALM 36: 7–9

Grace is given free of charge. Otherwise it is not grace. When Bonhoeffer coins the term "cheap grace", he is addressing the consequences of grace. He is living in Nazi Germany. The official Evangelical Church has accepted Nazism. They preach about grace every Sunday. In a formal, literal sense their preaching is correct. But it has no consequences. Grace is handed out without anyone standing up for those who are being executed for their heritage, convictions, or sexual orientation.

This causes Bonhoeffer to react adamantly: "Cheap grace is the deadly enemy of our Church. We are fighting today for costly grace. Cheap grace means grace sold on the market like cheapjacks' wares. The sacraments, the forgiveness of sin, and the consolations of religion are thrown away at cut prices. Grace is represented as the Church's inexhaustible treasury, from which she showers blessings with generous hands, without asking questions or fixing limits."

This representation of grace destroys, poisons, undermines everything the Church stands for. Cheap grace says yes to the sin, not to the sinner. Cheap grace turns grace into a doctrine, a theory—interesting to listen to, but without any real meaning.

In a sense it is true that God offers grace unconditionally. To understand the difference between cheap and costly grace, however, we can look to Faust. Towards the end of his life, having hungered for knowledge his whole life, he says, "Now I see that we know nothing finally". His insight is a conclusion. But if we make it our starting point, a premise, the statement has quite different implications. If a new student said the same thing, it might be a sign of laziness.

Grace is not something we can take for granted; it is something that is offered to us.

Grace is given, free of charge, to those who long for it. This is costly grace. If grace is seen as a given, a free pass that allows for any kind of life, it is a form of self-deception.

PRAYER

Teach me, God, to long for your grace,
costly and liberating.
Your grace gives me life.

23. The Polyphony of Life

LETTER TO EBERHARD BETHGE, 20 MAY 1944

> Above all, maintain constant love for one another, for love
> covers a multitude of sins. Be hospitable to one another
> without complaining. Like good stewards of the manifold
> grace of God, serve one another with whatever gift each
> of you has received.
>
> 1 PETER 4:8–10

A human life is diverse, a complex tapestry of so many colours it is not always easy to see it clearly. Our world consists of billions of people with unique personalities, each with their own individual imprint. And if we look closer at one single person, we discover so many features that we are easily overwhelmed. All of creation is made up of one vast plurality. Bonhoeffer calls this "the polyphony of life", using a musical term that describes a combination of several melody lines or voices.

Is it possible for one single feeling to take over and, as it were, push everything else aside—for instance, when two people share the powerful feeling of erotic love? Bonhoeffer addresses these thoughts in a letter to his newly-wed friend who, due to the war, had to live far away from his wife. Can the separation cause his friend to think so much about his beloved that he forgets all else? In the Song of Songs we read descriptions of glowing sensual love, far from any conservative norms of restrained emotions. It is remarkable that the Bible contains a text like the Song of Songs.

We can learn more about the multifaceted nature of life through musical terminology. The term *cantus firmus* refers to the base melody of a polyphonic composition. The other melody lines relate to this base as a counterpoint. We might say that our love for God is a *cantus firmus*, while our erotic love for another person is one of its counterpoints. In this sense, erotic love cannot possibly take up too much space. It must be allowed to play out its melody wholeheartedly and independently, but always in relation to the *cantus firmus*.

The love of God contains all earthly love; it encourages and permits all earthly love. Together they form a great polyphonic masterpiece, which plays throughout the day and throughout the night.

PRAYER

Teach me, God, to see the diversity
of life as a precious gift.

24. "We should find God in what we know, not in what we don't know"

LETTER TO EBERHARD BETHGE, 29 MAY 1944

> We love because God first loved us. Those who say "I love God", and hate their brothers or sisters, are liars; for those who do not love a brother or sister whom they have seen, cannot love God whom they have not seen.
>
> 1 JOHN 4:19-20

Humankind can get along fine without God. This is what more and more people think. The move towards human independence has been going on for a long time. Now we take it for granted in almost all parts of society. God is losing ground.

From a Christian perspective this development has been criticized as the great lapse from God. The movement towards human autonomy has been labelled "secularization", a term perceived as something negative, a threat to Christianity.

The defenders of the Christian faith seem to think that "the utmost questions" of death and guilt, at least, remain in the religious realm. The assumption is that only God can provide answers to these questions. God exists in order to clarify the greatest mysteries of life. God is seen as an emergency aid in situations when all else fails. But what happens if our greatest questions cease to exist or if they can be answered without the help of God?

Bonhoeffer looks at this image of God in which God can only mean something to people when they are burdened by guilt, fear of dying, and questions about the meaning of life. This image encourages people to see their happiness as their unhappiness, their health as their ailment, their vitality as their desperation.

"It has again brought home to me quite clearly that we shouldn't think of God as the stopgap for the incompleteness of our knowledge, because then—as is objectively inevitable—when the boundaries of knowledge are pushed ever further, God too is pushed further away and thus is ever on the retreat. We should find God in what we know, not in what we don't know."

Jesus did not begin by turning everyone into sinners. He met people as they were and gave them life regardless of their health or happiness.

A Christian faith offers a trust in God in all parts of life. It is not a belief in a power that sorts out the parts of life that humankind has not yet grasped. It is a faith in God as life itself, a God that lives with us in everything.

PRAYER

Teach me, God, to live as your friend, loving all people, trusting in your care for every one of us.

25. "Let him who cannot be alone beware of community"

LIFE TOGETHER, P. 57

> Now when Jesus heard this, he withdrew from there in a
> boat to a deserted place by himself.
>
> MATTHEW 14:13

We are born alone and we die alone. We struggle alone. We are alone in our life's most important decisions: we pray and hope, we fall in love, we choose what path to take. We should not fear being alone; it comes with being human. It is a place of freedom where we can come face to face with ourselves, life, and God. If we resist being alone, we risk losing out on life.

Sometimes we are afraid of being confronted by our deepest problems when we are alone. We escape to other people, hoping to find fellowship and understanding. But we are often disappointed and start blaming other people for what is really our own inner fear.

Christian community is not a "spiritual sanatorium". Someone who misuses community to escape from herself and her emptiness can easily end up facing greater isolation.

Through being alone we learn to appreciate ourselves and others, and we become open to community and fellowship. This is why being alone and being in a community are so closely linked. They go hand in hand, and one does not precede the other. They belong together and give us the freedom to be who we are.

On their own, being alone and being together can be sources of temptation. Community without space for being alone is characterized by empty talk, emotional overload, and spiritual platitudes. Being alone without community can easily reduce life so that it becomes meaningless, self-centred and desolate.

This goes for everyone, including followers of Christ. We need to practise being alone with ourselves, getting to know ourselves, making friends with ourselves. To meet ourselves, honestly and without deception, step by step. None of us fully knows who we are. Only God can truly know us.

Being alone enables us to be part of a vibrant community, where we can live out our loving kindness and our joy in being together.

PRAYER

Grant me, God, the courage to be alone with myself,
so that I may be your friend and worker
in human fellowship.
Help me to hold on to your presence in everything.

26. The Gift of Silence

A time to keep silence, and a time to speak.

ECCLESIASTES 3:7

Silence is a gift that opens doors to life. Regular times of silence allow words to grow at their own pace. "None speaketh surely but he that would gladly keep silence if he might", writes Thomas à Kempis, quoted by Bonhoeffer. It is not so much a case of keeping quiet, but more a receiving of silence as a gift before God.

We all step into silence when we go to sleep at night, and we wake up from our silence after our rest. We take these times of silence for granted. But both of these daily quiet times offer an opportunity to be with God, to hear the voice of God.

Silence can be misused. It can be a frightening wasteland of desolation and anxiety. Or it can be turned into a deceptive paradise, an escape from reality. These forms of silence are not what we are aiming at.

Silence can also be misused as a holier-than-thou, condescending attitude towards others. It is a hurtful, self-righteous sort of silence.

We must also distinguish holding silence from being muted. Being made mute is an imposed, ordered, and forceful silence. Silence and muteness are related, like true communication and empty talk. Silence is a gift that opens paths to life and allows words to appear. Silence for the friends of Jesus is a quiet waiting on God.

Morning prayer gives me words to shape and form my day. Evening prayer concludes my day and gathers the threads of my life. Prayer grows from silence. Prayer is a place in which we stand before the face of God. Prayer opens an inner space.

Silence, then, is connected to God's wishes for my life. But Christ's followers do not place any demands on silence. I do not need to expect anything special from it or hope for transforming experiences through it. Silence is liberating in itself as a gift from God. All that is required of us in our silence is to be there and to receive.

Silence reminds us of the very foundation of human life: to receive and to give. In that order. God gives and I receive, in order to give to others. But it all begins with receiving.

PRAYER

Teach me, God, how to receive silence as a gift from you,
where I may open myself, naked and undisguised.

27. Living in the this-worldliness of life

LETTER TO EBERHARD BETHGE, 21 JULY 1944

Thus says the LORD: [. . .] And you, do you seek great things for yourself? Do not seek them.

JEREMIAH 45:5

"I want to become a saint," said the young French priest in a conversation with Bonhoeffer in the early 1930s in America. The two young theologians were talking about their future. But they saw things differently. The French priest—whose name we now know is Jean Lasserre—made an impression on Bonhoeffer, but Bonhoeffer reacted to what he said, even then. Thirteen years later Bonhoeffer is sitting in cell 92 in the Tegel interrogation prison in Berlin. He recalls his conversation with Lasserre.

Now Bonhoeffer takes a clear stance against setting a goal for his future. Instead, he advocates living the earthly life we have been given as a gift from God, and to do so with all our heart. Our task is not to gaze towards a future where something else awaits us. If we do, we risk underestimating the challenges at hand, everything that calls for our immediate attention and commitment. The present moment is so vast and so immanent that it demands our full attention.

"If one has completely renounced making something of oneself—whether it be a saint or a converted sinner or a church leader (a so-called priestly figure!), a just or an unjust person, a sick or a healthy person—then one throws oneself completely into the arms of God, and this is what I call this-worldliness: living fully in the midst of life's tasks, questions, successes and failures, experiences, and perplexities."

Living here and now, in the this-worldliness of life, is to throw oneself into God's embrace. It is to live before God fully committed to the things that call for our attention and consideration, right now.

In doing so we live in solidarity with the people who are most in need, sharing in, to use Bonhoeffer's words, "God's suffering in the life of this world". In being present, we stay awake with Christ in Gethsemane—this is what faith is about, this is what it is to be human, to be a Christian.

When I let go of my struggle for personal greatness, I can take on the challenges that face me, I can take in the reality of life. I begin, truly and fully, to live my life. My life's goal is not to become more holy, more pious, greater or more saintly than everyone around me. This temptation leads me away from my life's true task: to live here and now for others.

PRAYER

God, grant me clarity from your clarity,
love from your love,
life from your life.

28. "God is weak and powerless in the world, and in precisely this way, and only so, is at our side and helps us"

LETTER TO EBERHARD BETHGE, 16 JULY 1944

> This was to fulfil what had been spoken through the prophet
> Isaiah, "He took our infirmities and bore our diseases."
>
> MATTHEW 8:17

When Bonhoeffer in his prison cell reflects on the help given to humans by God through a Christian faith, he considers the powerlessness of God. We might have imagined he would rather have looked for Bible passages that emphasize God's strength. Bonhoeffer himself is a victim of an inhumane political power that incessantly diminishes and denies human worth. The idea of a God that displays power by intervening in the world's power structures and imposing justice must be tempting.

But Bonhoeffer seeks the absolute opposite image of God. When God is powerless, God is greatest. It is through suffering that Christ is closest to us. "[God] gains ground and power in the world by being powerless", he writes in the letter cited in the title. The God we read about in our Bible is not one that solves problems, intervenes, and makes everything better. Instead it is only the powerless, suffering God that can help people. It is in weakness that God is closest to us.

But it is not an appeasing sort of weakness that makes people feel sorry for themselves. It is a closeness to life itself.

In our weakness we are closer to ourselves and to God. In our weakness we clearly see that human life is greater than everything we can dominate and control. We do not own our own life. Our life belongs to God who has given life to all of creation. In our weakness we see that the greatest things in life are the most fragile things, the things that could so easily break but endure everything. We might think of falling in love—so tender and fragile, yet so strong. We might think of friendship, faith, tenderness, relationships—everything that can so easily be turned into its opposite.

When we are truly close to life itself, human weakness is exposed, the same weakness that is our strength. When we are truly close to life, we are truly close to God.

PRAYER

God, show me how to find safety in the fragility of life,
where you live with me always.

29. "With God we live without God"

LETTER TO EBERHARD BETHGE, 16 JULY 1944

At three o'clock Jesus cried out with a loud voice, "Eloi, Eloi, lema sabachtani?" which means, "My God, my God, why have you forsaken me?"

MARK 15:34

There is a sheer honesty in the stories about Jesus. At times they are so raw we have trouble taking them in. One of these moments is the desperate cry from Jesus on the cross that God has forsaken him. We find the same account from two apostles, Matthew and Mark, which makes the story historically credible.

But what does it really mean? Bonhoeffer is a man who seeks an honest answer. His view is that the God who is with us is the God who leaves us. We must learn to live "as if there were no God". We must take responsibility for our own life, our actions, our words.

God makes this clear to us. God wants us to live as humans who can manage without God—we must do this before God and with God.

In times of trouble and uncertainty, we can express our thoughts in prayer to God. But it is essentially I, and I alone, who must make the final decisions, take a stand, choose a path.

This has not always been emphasized in the Christian tradition. People have spoken of "spiritual guidance" as a way of legitimizing a decision. In reality this language has been an attempt at decorating a person's own choice with a pious and even authoritarian gloss.

But God has created us as responsible individuals who must shape our lives from the resources given to us. There is no divine guide pointing us in the right direction, nor do we have the luxury of some divine washerwoman who cleans up our mess. We have been given life as a gift from God in order to live it and shape it ourselves, fully responsible for our own lives and for the people who are affected by our choices.

We must do this trusting that we live each day and night before the face of God. We must do this believing that God will remain with us to the end of time.

PRAYER

Help me, God, to live before you and with you,
and even when I feel forsaken and alone.

30. "Jesus calls not to a new religion but to life"

LETTER TO EBERHARD BETHGE, 18 JULY 1944

Jesus said to him, "I am the way, and the truth, and the life."

JOHN 14:6

For two thousand years people have asked questions about Jesus, about his deeds and his words. For two thousand years people have called themselves friends of Jesus and wanted to belong to his community of friends. The conditions of calling yourself a friend of Jesus have changed throughout history. In some cases the demands have been so specific that it is hard to see how Christians relate to non-Christians at all.

It is true that Christians have often tried to isolate themselves, build walls around themselves, and protect themselves from the influence of those who do not belong to the Christian community. But I think there are more cases in which followers of Jesus seek fellowship with people regardless of creed and convictions. This has happened in different ways, I know. The fundamental fellowship of humankind is a fundamental feature of the Christian belief in creation.

What we call religion has often had a divisive effect. The term religion is not very old; it goes back only a few hundred years. But it has almost always been used to separate groups of faith: Christians from Jews, Christians from Muslims,

Christians from Hindus and Buddhists, and Christians from those without faith.

In this context, Bonhoeffer's words are absolutely radical. Jesus has not come to call for a new religion, to create yet another closed group of people with their own set of views.

Jesus has come to call people to live a full life. What is at stake is the life given to every person at birth. Everything that Jesus says and does is aimed at making this earthly life a full life, a true life, a life in which people live for one another.

And the arsenal of instruments and tools developed by the Christian Church throughout history has the same aim: to enable people to live life fully and wholeheartedly, to live close to the main artery of life, close to life itself.

PRAYER

God, you who have given me life,
help me to hold on to you, giver of life.
Only when I trust in you who gives life,
do I realize that my life is greater
than I can ever comprehend.

Christian and Heathens

People go to God when they're in need,
plead for help, pray for blessings and bread,
for rescue from their sickness, guilt, and death.
So do they all. all of them, Christians and heathens.

People go to God when God's in need,
find God poor, reviled, without shelter or bread,
see God devoured by sin, weakness, and death.
Christians stand by God in God's own pain.

God goes to all people in their need,
fills body and soul with God's own bread,
goes for Christians and heathens to Calvary's death
and forgives them both.

FROM *LETTERS AND PAPERS FROM PRISON*

By gracious powers so wonderfully sheltered

By gracious powers so wonderfully sheltered,
and confidently waiting come what may,
we know that God is with us night and morning,
and never fails to greet us each new day.

Yet is this heart by its old foe tormented,
still evil days bring burdens hard to bear.
O, give our frightened souls the sure salvation
for which, O Lord, You taught us to prepare.

And when this cup You give is filled to brimming
with bitter suffering, hard to understand,
we take it thankfully and without trembling,
out of so good, and so beloved, a hand.

Yet when again in, this same world, you give us
the joy we had, the brightness of your sun,
we shall remember all the days we lived through,
and our whole life shall then be yours alone.

FRED PRATT GREEN (1903–2000) LOOSELY BASED
ON THE GERMAN OF DIETRICH BONHOEFFER

References

The English rendition of the Dietrich Bonhoeffer texts uses the following translations:

Bonhoeffer, Dietrich, *Letters and Papers from Prison*, trans. Isabel Best *et al.*, (Minneapolis: Fortress Press, 2015).

Bonhoeffer, Dietrich, *Life Together*, trans. John W. Doberstein, (London: SCM Press Ltd, 1954).

Bonhoeffer, Dietrich, *The Cost of Discipleship*, trans. R. H. Fuller (London: SCM Press Ltd, 1959).

The Bible texts are taken from the New Revised Standard Version: Anglicized Edition (Oxford University Press).

Lightning Source UK Ltd.
Milton Keynes UK
UKHW022056050119
334983UK00003B/94/P

9 781910 519936